Great Women
of the Bible

The Wives of King David, Jezebel,
The Shunammite Woman, Esther

CONCORDIA PUBLISHING HOUSE • SAINT LOUIS

Copyright © 2008 Concordia Publishing House
3558 S. Jefferson Ave., St. Louis, MO 63118-3968
1-800-325-3040 • www.cph.org

Scripture quotations are from The Holy Bible, English Standard Version®. Copyright © 2001 by Crossway Bibles, a publishing ministry of Good News Publishers, Wheaton, Illinois. Used by permission. All rights reserved.

Hymn texts with the abbreviation *LSB* are from *Lutheran Service Book*, copyright © 2006 by Concordia Publishing House. All rights reserved.

This publication may be available in braille, in large print, or on cassette tape for the visually impaired. Please allow 8 to 12 weeks for delivery. Write to Lutheran Blind Mission, 7550 Watson Rd., St. Louis, MO 63119-4409; call toll-free 1-888-215-2455; or visit the Web site: www.blindmission.org.

Manufactured in the United States of America

1 2 3 4 5 6 7 8 9 10   17 16 15 14 13 12 11 10 09 08

Contents

Hymnal Key

LSB = Lutheran Service Book
ELH = Evangelical Lutheran Hymnary
CW = Christian Worship
LW = Lutheran Worship
LBW = Lutheran Book of Worship
TLH = The Lutheran Hymnal

About This Series

Do you realize how often women are mentioned in the Bible? Do names like Eve, Sarah, Deborah, Ruth, Esther, Mary the mother of Jesus, Anna, Mary and Martha, Lydia, and Eunice and Lois sound familiar? They should. These are only a few of the great women mentioned in Holy Scripture.

The Bible not only gives us the names of these great women, but also describes their sorrows and joys, their defeats and victories, their intense private moments and important public duties. In contrast to the inaccurate myth that the Bible is an antiquated piece of antiwoman (misogynistic) literature, the Bible portrays women as God's creatures, different yet fully equal with men, fallen in sin yet redeemed by the precious blood of the Lamb.

In addition to sharing the thoughts, dreams, words, and deeds of women in the past, the Bible also provides helpful instruction for women of today. It encourages thrift and industry (Proverbs 31:10–31), teaches about healthy relationships between husbands and wives (Ephesians 5:22–33; Colossians 3:18–19), provides instruction in the relationship between older and younger women (Titus 2:3–5), celebrates the equality in diversity among believers (Galatians 3:28–29), and extols the important and varied roles women play in the partnership of the Gospel (Philippians 4:3).

Women can learn much about themselves in the Bible. But it would be a mistake to assume that what the Bible teaches about women is of no importance to men. In His Word, God unfolds for the believer both true womanhood and true manhood as He designed them, so that both sexes are affirmed in their equality and in their differences as God created them.

In this series, we cannot learn all there is to know about every great woman of the Bible. However, as we study His Word, we can learn much about ourselves, our Lord, and His saving grace.

Suggestions for Small-Group Participants

1. Before you begin, spend some time in prayer, asking God to strengthen your faith through a study of His Word. The Scriptures were written so that we might believe in Jesus Christ and have life in His name (John 20:31).

2. Even if you are not the small-group leader, take some time prior to the meeting to look over the session, read the Bible verses, and answer the questions.

3. As a courtesy to others, be sure to arrive at each session on time.

4. Be an active participant. The leader will facilitate group discussion, not give a lecture.

5. Avoid dominating the conversation by answering each question or by giving unnecessarily long answers. Avoid the temptation to not share at all.

6. Treat anything shared in your group as confidential until you have asked for and received permission to share it outside of the group. Treat information about others outside of your group as confidential until you have asked for and received permission to share it inside of your group.

7. Realize that some participants may be new to the group or new to the Christian faith. Help them to feel welcomed and comfortable.

8. Affirm other participants when you can. If another participant offers what you perceive to be a "wrong" answer, ask the Holy Spirit to guide that person to seek the correct answer from God's Word.

9. Keep in mind that the questions are discussion starters. Don't be afraid to ask additional questions that relate to the session. Avoid getting the group off track.

10. If you feel comfortable doing so, now and then volunteer to pray either at the beginning or at the conclusion of the session.

Suggestions for Small-Group Leaders

1. Before you begin, spend some time in prayer asking God to strengthen your faith through a study of His Word. The Scriptures were written so that we might believe in Jesus Christ and have life in His name (John 20:31). Also, pray for participants by name.

2. See the Leader Guide at the back of this study. It will help guide you in discovering the truths of God's Word. It is not, however, exhaustive, nor is it designed to be read aloud during your session.

3. Prior to your meeting, familiarize yourself with each session by reviewing the session material, reading the Bible passages, and answering the questions in the spaces provided. Your familiarity with the session will give you confidence as you lead the group.

4. As a courtesy to participants, begin and end each session on time.

5. Have a Bible dictionary or similar resource handy in order to look up difficult or unfamiliar names, words, and places. Ask participants to help you in this task. Be sure that each participant has a Bible and a study guide.

6. Ask for volunteers to read introductory paragraphs and Bible passages. A simple "thank you" will encourage them to volunteer again.

7. See your role as a conversation facilitator rather than a lecturer. Don't be afraid to give participants time to answer questions. By name, thank each participant who answers; then ask for other participants. For example, you may say, "Thank you, Maggie. Would anyone else like to share?"

8. Now and then, summarize aloud what the group has learned by studying God's Word.

9. Keep in mind that the questions provided are discussion starters. Allow participants to ask questions that relate to the session. However, keep discussions on track with the session.

10. Everyone is a learner! If you don't know the answer to a question, simply tell participants that you need time to look at more Scripture passages or to ask your pastor, director of Christian education, or other lay leader. You can provide an answer at the next session.

11. Begin each session with prayer. Conclude each session with prayer. Ask for volunteers for these duties, and thank them for their participation. A suggested hymn is included at the end of each session. You may choose another hymn or song if you wish.

12. Encourage participants to read or reread the Scripture passages provided at the end of the session and, as they have time, to commit passages to memory.

The Wives of King David

David was the greatest statesman and ruler of the Hebrew nation. His reign and that of his son Solomon are regarded as the golden age of Israel's history. The Bible points particularly to David as one of the greatest heroes of faith; it calls him a man after the heart of God because of his piety and religious zeal. In fact, the name *Son of David* was to be applied to the Messiah as a title of honor.

We should familiarize ourselves also with the women who played important roles in David's life. As we have seen in this series, great women in the Bible had both strengths and weaknesses, yet God used them for His gracious purposes. In this section, we will probably not find a satisfactory answer to explain David's many marital relationships, but we will learn a lot about the kind of women David married. Three women, in particular, played a prominent part in David's life.

Michal

Although King Saul had promised to give David his eldest daughter, Merab, in marriage (1 Samuel 18:17), David remained humble, even as Saul went back on his word (vv. 18–19). In deceit, Saul later offered David the hand of Michal, who was in love with David (vv. 20–21). David finally agreed to Saul's request (v. 26).

1. What do you think of such a marriage? How was David treated by his father-in-law (1 Samuel 19:10)?

Learning of Saul's plan to kill her husband, Michal saved David's life by warning him against the plot. Her deception included pretending before her own father that an idol in David's bed was a sick David (see 1 Samuel 19:11–17).

2. What would you have done in this situation had you been Michal? Does 1 Samuel 18:20 help explain her actions?

As ruler, Saul legitimately dissolved Michal's marriage to David by giving her to Paltiel, or Palti (1 Samuel 25:44). David later broke up this marriage so that Michal could live with him again as his wife (2 Samuel 3:13–16).

3. How would you describe Michal's relationship with David (2 Samuel 6:16; 20–23)? Do you think that Michal would have been better off had she never married David?

Abigail

Abigail's first husband was Nabal, who "was harsh and badly behaved" (1 Samuel 25:3). David was determined to kill Nabal because although Nabal was rich, he refused to offer hospitality to David and his men (vv. 5–13).

4. How did Abigail's servant show that his mistress was exceedingly wise and could be trusted (vv. 14–17)? What did Abigail do to prevent David from committing murder (vv. 18–31)?

Abigail waited until Nabal was sober before telling him of her dealings with David. Upon hearing the news, Nabal apparently had a stroke and died (see 1 Samuel 25:36–38).

5. With her husband dead, David offered to marry Abigail. She consented (vv. 39–42). What lesson might Abigail teach women who are unhappily married?

Bathsheba

One of the most famous—and most shameful—love stories in the Bible is the story of David and Bathsheba. David is to be faulted for initiating his adulterous relationship with Bathsheba (2 Samuel 11:1–5), which included placing her husband, Uriah, in death's way (vv. 14–15, 26).

6. Although David confessed his sin and was absolved (2 Samuel 12:1–13), God allowed Bathsheba and David's first child to die (vv. 14, 18). Why does God sometimes allow us to suffer the temporal results of our sins?

Later, God blessed Bathsheba and David with another son, Solomon (2 Samuel 12:24). Solomon honored his mother, the queen mother, while she was alive (see 1 Kings 2:19–20).

7. What even greater honor did God bestow upon Bathsheba (Matthew 1:6)?

Other Women of That Period

8. Who were some of David's many other wives (1 Chronicles 3:1–9)?

9. How did Solomon demonstrate God's wisdom when called upon to settle a quarrel between two women (1 Kings 3:16–28)?

10. What practical advantage was there for Solomon to marry an Egyptian princess (1 Kings 3:1)? What special honor did he bestow upon her (7:8)?

11. Whom did the Queen of Sheba praise for Solomon's great wisdom and wealth (see 1 Kings 10:1–10, especially v. 9)? What did Jesus say about her (Matthew 12:42)?

12. Solomon's multiple marriages led to an increase of idolatry in Israel (1 Kings 11:1–11). Why should we be especially careful of the spiritual company we keep?

Closing Worship

Close by reading or singing together the words of "Renew Me, O Eternal Light" (*LSB* 704; *LW* 373; *TLH* 398; *CW* 471; *LBW* 511).

Renew me, O eternal Light,
And let my heart and soul be bright,
Illumined with the light of grace
That issues from Your holy face.

Remove the pow'r of sin from me
And cleanse all my impurity
That I may have the strength and will

Temptations of the flesh to still.
Create in me a new heart, Lord,
That gladly I obey Your Word.
Let what You will be my desire,
And with new life my soul inspire.

Grant that I only You may love
And seek those things which are above
Till I behold You face to face,
O Light eternal, through Your grace.

Johann Friedrich Ruopp, 1672–1708; tr. August Crull, 1845–1923, alt.
Public domain

For Daily Devotions or Bible Reading

Monday: 1 Samuel 18–19
Tuesday: 1 Samuel 25
Wednesday: 2 Samuel 3:1–16; 6:12–23
Thursday: 2 Samuel 11–12
Friday: 2 Samuel 13
Saturday: 1 Kings 1:1–2:25; 3:16–28
Sunday: 1 Kings 10:1–13; 2 Chronicles 9:1–12
For memorization: Psalm 51:1–12; Matthew 12:42

✑
Jezebel

The Bible tells us not only about great women of faith but also about women who were very wicked and cruel. God tells us about such people in order to warn us against becoming like them (1 Corinthians 10:6, 11–12). Their lives serve as examples of how dangerous it is to take sin lightly.

In the story of the prophet Elijah, we come across two people who caused God's prophet a great deal of trouble: Jezebel and her husband, Ahab. It has been said that Jezebel is the wickedest woman in the Bible. Ordinarily, we would not want to learn anything about such a person. However, we can still learn from Jezebel how bad life can become when a woman has no place for God in her heart or life.

The Pagan Queen of Israel

Jezebel was the daughter of Ethbaal, king of the Sidonians, who were Baal worshipers (1 Kings 16:31). Ahab, king of Israel, married Jezebel.

13. Why was the marriage between Jezebel and Ahab not surprising (vv. 30, 32–33)? In what way were the people of Israel affected by this marriage?

Jezebel and Ahab hated Elijah, the Lord's prophet, because the Lord had sent a drought and because of Elijah's preaching (1 Kings 17:1; 18:1–17).

14. To what extent had Jezebel tried to turn God's people away from Him to her false god (18:13, 19)?

God's dramatic victory on Mount Carmel over the priests of Baal failed to impress Queen Jezebel (1 Kings 19:1–2). Even after such a display of God's power, Elijah feared for his life (v. 3).

15. In spite of Jezebel's cruelty, God promised that His Church would survive (19:18). What comfort can we take from Jesus' promise about His Church (Matthew 16:18)?

The Murderess of Naboth

Ahab wanted to procure a vineyard owned by Naboth, a Jezreelite, because it was located near Ahab's house. In exchange, Ahab was willing to trade another vineyard for Naboth's or pay him a fair price for it (see 1 Kings 21:1–4).

16. Why could Naboth not sell it to him (v. 3; see also Numbers 36:7)? What was Ahab's reaction when Naboth declined his offer (v. 4)?

Jezebel deceitfully schemed to have Naboth killed in order to secure Naboth's vineyard for her husband (vv. 5–14).

17. What sins did Jezebel commit? Why do you think Ahab capitulated to Jezebel's plans? What happened after Naboth's death (vv. 15–16)?

Impenitent to Her End

Elijah prophesied a horrible death for Jezebel (1 Kings 21:23), a prophecy that ultimately was fulfilled (2 Kings 9:30–37).

18. To her tragic end, Jezebel remained hardened in sin and unbelief (see 2 Kings 9:30). The Lord doesn't desire, however, "that any should perish, but that all should reach repentance" (2 Peter 3:9). How can we Christians make the most of the Lord's generous desire to forgive us of our sins?

19. Another Jezebel appears in Revelation 2:20. In his *Revelation* commentary, Louis A. Brighton suggests that this Jezebel represents religious syncretism, the belief that all religions, including Christianity, are of equal value. What steps could we take to avoid this modern Jezebel?

Other Women of That Period

King Jeroboam sent his wife on a sad mission to learn from the Lord's priest, Ahijah, that their child would die as a result of Jeroboam's many sins (1 Kings 14:1–18). In His mercy, God would allow the child to be buried (v. 13).

20. What comfort do Christian parents have when death takes their child? What can your congregation do to help parents who lose children and to help children who lose siblings?

The story of the widow of Zarephath is a story of God's great comfort and care for the needy. Even though she was a pagan, the prophet Elijah performed two miracles for her and her son (1 Kings 17:8–24).

21. What were the two miracles? What use did Jesus make of her story (Luke 4:25–26)?

Closing Worship

Close by reading or singing together the words of "Jesus Sinners Doth Receive" (*LSB* 609; *LW* 229; *TLH* 324; *CW* 304; *LBW* 291).

Jesus sinners doth receive;
    Oh, may all this saying ponder
Who in sin's delusions live
    And from God and heaven wander!
Here is hope for all who grieve:
Jesus sinners doth receive.

We deserve but grief and shame,
    Yet His words, rich grace revealing,
Pardon, peace, and life proclaim;
    Here our ills have perfect healing.
Firmly in these words believe:
Jesus sinners doth receive.

Sheep that from the fold did stray
    No true shepherd e'er forsaketh;
Weary souls that lost their way
    Christ, the Shepherd, gently taketh
In His arms that they may live:
Jesus sinners doth receive.

I, a sinner, come to Thee
    With a penitent confession.
Savior, mercy show to me;
    Grant for all my sins remission.
Let these words my soul relieve:
Jesus sinners doth receive.

Oh, how blest it is to know:
  Were as scarlet my transgression,
It shall be as white as snow
  By Thy blood and bitter passion;
For these words I now believe:
Jesus sinners doth receive.

Now my conscience is at peace;
  From the Law I stand acquitted.
Christ hath purchased my release
  And my ev'ry sin remitted.
Naught remains my soul to grieve:
Jesus sinners doth receive.

Jesus sinners doth receive;
  Also I have been forgiven;
And when I this earth must leave,
  I shall find an open heaven.
Dying, still to Him I cleave:
Jesus sinners doth receive.

Erdmann Neumeister, 1671–1756; tr. *The Lutheran Hymnal*, 1941, alt.
Public domain

For Daily Devotions or Bible Reading

Monday: 1 Kings 14:1–20; 16:29–34
Tuesday: 1 Kings 17
Wednesday: 1 Kings 18
Thursday: 1 Kings 19
Friday: 1 Kings 21
Saturday: 2 Kings 9
Sunday: 2 Kings 11; Psalm 73
For memorization: Numbers 32:23; Psalm 73:3, 12, 16–18

The Shunammite Woman

Not all the great women of the Bible who faithfully served the Lord and His Church are mentioned by name. But the Lord knows them, and their names are recorded in heaven (see 2 Timothy 2:19; Philippians 4:3). On earth, their faith and their lives are more important to us than their names, which we will learn in heaven.

What the Bible tells us about these great women is to encourage us to follow their example and glorify God in our daily lives. The woman whose life we will now study is known only by the place where she lived. Her home was at Shunem, a little town in Galilee about 5 miles from Mount Tabor. The Shunammite woman is a wonderful example of a person of faith who by her good works proved that she was a true child of God.

A Woman of Hospitality

The Shunammite woman was wealthy and generous. Whenever the Lord's prophet, Elisha, would come to town, she would feed him. Eventually, she persuaded her husband to allow a small apartment to be constructed on their roof for Elisha's comfort (2 Kings 4:8–11).

22. Why do you suppose the woman became interested in Elisha (see v. 9)?

23. What may we also learn from her about showing hospitality to and providing for the needs of our pastors, teachers, deaconesses, missionaries, and other church workers?

Elisha offered to repay the Shunammite woman's kindness by speaking well of her to the king or the commander of the army (vv. 11–13). But she had no need of such special favors.

24. Instead, how did Elisha prove to her that God rewards those who honor His servants (vv. 15–17)? Is this true even today (Matthew 10:40–42)?

A Woman Who Believed in God's Promise

Later, the Shunammite's child died. The Shunammite traveled on a donkey some four hours (about 16 miles) to Mount Carmel in order to get Elisha to return with her to heal her son (2 Kings 4:18–37).

25. How are we to explain the Shunammite's remark to Elisha that all was well at her house (v. 26)? To whom should we Christians turn when we are faced with sadness, illness, or death?

26. How did Elisha restore the Shunammite's son to life (vv. 33–35)? How did she show her thankfulness to God for this miracle (v. 37)? List some ways we can show thankfulness to our Christian sisters and brothers when they help us in our time of need.

A Woman Who Experienced God's Help

Elisha proved to be a true friend to the Shunammite, caring both about her spiritual and her temporal concerns. Gehazi, Elisha's servant, sought to secure her property and goods following a seven-year absence (2 Kings 8:1–6).

27. Elisha warned the Shunammite of a coming famine and to seek refuge and sustenance elsewhere (vv. 1–2). In what ways can your congregation be concerned about the physical well-being of your congregational members? community members?

28. Following her seven-year absence because of the famine, Gehazi appealed to the king on her behalf. As a result, the Shunammite's property and rights were restored (vv. 3–6). In what ways can your congregation be an advocate for those seeking justice or fair treatment under the law?

Other Women of That Period

One of the prophets' widows appealed to Elisha out of her extreme poverty. She possessed only a jar of oil. God through Elisha provided a great miracle by multiplying the oil that the widow had so that she could sell the oil and provide income for herself and her two children (2 Kings 4:1–7).

29. List resources your congregation, women's groups, or other groups currently provide or can provide to assist those suffering from poverty and want.

A young Hebrew girl bravely witnessed to the power of God by telling her mistress about God's prophet, Elisha. Because of her testimony, Naaman, her mistress's husband, would eventually be cleansed of leprosy by bathing in the Jordan (2 Kings 5:1–14).

30. What can we Christians learn about personal evangelism from this young girl? Discuss opportunities you have for winning unbelievers for Christ.

31. Jezebel's daughter, Athaliah, was cruel like her mother and like her met a sad end (2 Kings 11:1–3, 13–16, 20). Discuss the importance of Christian parents modeling proper behavior, attitudes, and speech before their children.

32. Considering that her husband was very wicked, Hezekiah's mother must have played a godly role in her son's life (2 Kings 18:1–7). Based on the behavior of Manasseh, could the same be said of Hezekiah's wife, Manasseh's mother (21:1–9)?

33. Among what special class of women is Huldah to be reckoned (2 Kings 22:14–20)?

Closing Worship

Close by reading or singing together the words of "Entrust Your Days and Burdens" (*LSB* 754; *LW* 427; *TLH* 520).

Entrust your days and burdens
    To God's most loving hand;
He cares for you while ruling
    The sky, the sea, the land.

For He who guides the tempests
  Along their thund'rous ways
Will find for you a pathway
  And guide you all your days.

Rely on God your Savior
  And find your life secure.
Make His work your foundation
  That your work may endure.
No anxious thought, no worry,
  No self-tormenting care
Can win your Father's favor;
  His heart is moved by prayer.

Take heart, have hope, my spirit,
  And do not be dismayed;
God helps in ev'ry trial
  And makes you unafraid.
Await His time with patience
  Through darkest hours of night
Until the sun you hoped for
  Delights your eager sight.

Leave all to His direction;
  His wisdom rules for you
In ways to rouse your wonder
  At all His love can do.
Soon He, His promise keeping,
  With wonder-working pow'rs
Will banish from your spirit
  What gave you troubled hours.

Paul Gerhardt, 1607–76; tr. F. Samuel Janzow, 1913–2001, alt..

For Daily Devotions or Bible Reading

Monday: 2 Kings 4
Tuesday: 2 Kings 5
Wednesday: 2 Kings 8
Thursday: 2 Kings 11
Friday: 2 Kings 18
Saturday: 2 Kings 22
Sunday: Ezra 9–10
For memorization: Hebrews 13:1, 7, 14, 16; John 11:25–26; 1 Peter 5:7

✑ Esther

The highest position of power and influence that any human being can hold in this world is to be the ruler of a mighty nation. As such, many people have become prominent on the pages of history. Historically, wives of great kings have generally been able to wield a tremendous influence over their ruling husbands for the good or evil of their people.

Even without a king, some queens have reigned successfully as the supreme rulers of their country or countries in their own right. We undoubtedly know of several queens who have made such a mark. However, when we think of queens in the Bible, the name that will probably first come to our minds is Queen Esther. She is the Hebrew girl who became the wife of the king of Persia.

Esther Becomes Queen

King Ahasuerus (Xerxes) ruled Persia at the time of our story (ca. 480 BC). Because of the disobedience of his current queen, the king sought to replace her (see Esther 1:1–2:4).

34. How do you think Mordecai felt about Esther, his cousin and ward, being taken to the king's harem (Esther 2:5–11)? What was Esther's Hebrew name (2:7)?

Because of her beauty and demeanor, Esther was elevated within Ahasuerus's harem (2:9). Eventually, as Esther's reputation and Ahasuerus's love for her grew, he crowned her queen (v. 17).

35. Why did Esther not tell the king that she was a Jewess (v. 20)? In what way did Mordecai, through Esther, preserve Ahasuerus's life (vv. 21–22)?

Esther's People Threatened with Destruction

Haman was a man appointed to a high position by King Ahasuerus. As vizier, Haman had great authority over all the empire. And yet, the refusal of one man to bow down to Haman ignited within him a burning anger against all of the Jews (Esther 3:1–5).

36. Describe Haman's plot against the Jews (vv. 6–11). Who else betrayed a Jew with pieces of silver (Matthew 26:14–16)?

Mordecai told Esther of Haman's evil plot against their people. Although initially reluctant to speak to the king about it (she risked her own life [Esther 4:11]), she consented to act on behalf of her people because of Mordecai's warning (4:1–14).

37. What risk was Esther now willing to take (vv. 15–17)? What stand should we Christians take when we must choose between doing what is right and looking out for our own interests?

Esther Saves Her People from Destruction

Donning her royal apparel, Esther won favorable attention from the king and was able to enter his presence (Esther 5:1–3).

38. How did Esther show great wisdom and shrewdness by not immediately telling the king of her predicament (vv. 4–8)? Why might she have invited the king and powerful Haman to two successive banquets (vv. 4, 8)?

Haman plotted to hang Mordecai (vv. 9–14). During the night, however, Ahasuerus couldn't sleep and had the book of memorable deeds read to him, during which he realized that Mordecai had never been properly honored for saving his life. Not knowing that the king had Mordecai in mind, Haman suggested a way to honor such a man (ch. 6). It is following the bestowal of this honor that we join the king, Haman, and Esther at Esther's feast.

39. How did Queen Esther reveal Haman's treachery to the king during the second day of the feast (7:1–6)? Ironically, what became of him (vv. 7–10)? What steps did the king take so that the law Haman had forced through could not be carried out (8:7–11)?

Esther Is Honored

Ahasuerus honored Mordecai by parading him through the city in royal robes (8:15–17) and by giving Mordecai great power (9:4), second only to the king himself (ch. 10).

40. How did the Jews celebrate the victory Esther had won for them (8:16–17)? Why were their enemies afraid to attack them (9:2–16)?

41. Why was the Purim festival instituted (9:21–22)? Explain what the name *pur* means. How was this festival celebrated (vv. 21–28)? Do Jewish people still observe this festival today?

42. Although God's name is not mentioned in the Book of Esther, His providential hand is evident throughout. So, too, are the faith-filled deeds of God's people. List how Mordecai and Esther demonstrated their obedient faith in our gracious God.

Other Women in the Book of Esther

43. Who was Queen Vashti, and why did she refuse to attend Ahasuerus's feast (Esther 1:9–12)? What eventually became of her (vv. 13–22)?

44. In the beginning, Zeresh, Haman's wife, supported Haman's opposition to Mordecai (Esther 5:14). How did her tune change once Mordecai had been given his royal parade (6:13)? Why is it important to be consistent in values and advice?

Closing Worship

Close by reading or singing together the words of "Take My Life and Let It Be" (*LSB* 783; *LW* 404; *TLH* 400; *CW* 469; *LBW* 406; *ELH* 444).

Take my life and let it be
Consecrated, Lord, to Thee;
Take my moments and my days,
Let them flow in ceaseless praise.

Take my hands and let them move
At the impulse of Thy love;
Take my feet and let them be
Swift and beautiful for Thee.

Take my voice and let me sing
Always, only for my King;
Take my lips and let them be
Filled with messages from Thee.

Take my silver and my gold,
Not a mite would I withhold;
Take my intellect and use
Ev'ry pow'r as Thou shalt choose.

Take my will and make it Thine,
It shall be no longer mine;
Take my heart, it is Thine own,
It shall be Thy royal throne.

Take my love, my Lord, I pour
At Thy feet its treasure store;
Take myself, and I will be
Ever, only, all for Thee.

Frances R. Havergal, 1836–79
Public domain

For Daily Devotions or Bible Reading

Monday: Esther 1
Tuesday: Esther 2
Wednesday: Esther 3
Thursday: Esther 4
Friday: Esther 5–6
Saturday: Esther 7–8
Sunday: Esther 9–10
For memorization: Proverbs 22:4, 29; 24:17, 19; Jeremiah
    29:7; 1 Timothy 2:1–3

Leader Guide

Each one-hour session is divided into three to six subsections. Participants will first look at the life of the historical figure in the biblical text. Then they will be encouraged from what they read and discuss to make practical application to their own lives and situations.

Remember that this study is only a guide. Your role as group leader is to facilitate interaction between individual participants and the biblical text and among participants in your small group. By God's Spirit working through His Word, participants will learn and grow together.

Begin and end each session with prayer. Each session concludes with suggestions for weekly Bible readings, Bible memorization, and a hymn. You may choose a different hymn or song based on the needs of your group.

The Wives of King David

The Bible introduces us to only three of David's wives. As we will see, each possessed a strong personality and exerted considerable influence upon him. The Bible does not tell us much about David's other wives except their names and the names of their children (e.g., see 1 Chronicles 3:1–9).

Michal

1. Previously known by Saul for his musical skills, David was still a very young man when he attracted the king's attention again by slaying Goliath (1 Samuel 17). Saul had promised to give his oldest daughter, Merab, to the man who would kill the giant (v. 25). But Saul did not keep his promise to David, because jealously he regarded David as his rival for the throne (1 Samuel 18:9–11, 17–19). Saul quickly married Merab to another man.

Since Saul was bent upon David's destruction, Michal's affection for David seemed to fit well into Saul's plans (vv. 20–21). He demanded a dowry from David that he believed David could not furnish without losing his life (v. 25). But to Saul's chagrin, David brought double the required gift and thereby increased his popularity with the people. Saul had to give his daughter to his enemy, but he hoped that she would help him carry out his schemes against David.

Allow participants to offer their views about such a marriage. Arranged marriages were typical at that time and place. In one particular incident, Saul showed his contempt for his son-in-law, perceiving him as a younger rival (1 Samuel 19:10).

2. Michal soon had opportunity to show that she had inherited her father's cunning (1 Samuel 19:11–17). But she used this for the benefit of her husband, whom she loved, and against her father, toward whom she had grown cold. Michal was probably convinced that David would eventually win out against Saul. She beat her father at his own game.

Allow participants to discuss what they might have done had they been in Michal's shoes. Certainly Michal's deep love for David (1 Samuel 18:20) motivated her to protect her husband and to deceive her father.

3. Saul punished Michal by forcing her to become the wife of Palti in distant Gallim (1 Samuel 25:44). Saul's act was tyrannical, but the king's rule was the law of the land. Hence, Michal's marriage to David was legally dissolved. David misused his regal authority, just as Saul had done; he should have let Palti keep Michal as his wife (2 Samuel 3:13–16).

Michal's love for David eventually grew cold. Perhaps she resented his other marriages and felt humiliated that her father's house had been wiped out. It must have hurt her deeply to be only a woman in David's harem and to have no son who could aspire to the throne. In 2 Samuel 6:16, 20–23, she shows how her lack of love had grown into bitterness. Both Michal and David lost their temper with each other and insulted each other. They inflicted verbal wounds that could not be healed.

Although it calls for pious speculation, allow participants to discuss whether Michal would have been better off if she hadn't married David.

Abigail

4. Abigail was a woman of fine character and outstanding talents. The Bible praises her wisdom and beauty (1 Samuel 25:3). Her husband, Nabal (which means "fool," v. 25), was wealthy, but he was selfish, stubborn, mean, and a drunkard. It was hard for any person to get along with him (v. 17). David had been kind to him, but when David asked for a few sheep to feed his hungry men, Nabal curtly refused to show gratitude toward his benefactor. Although Abigail was unhappy, she remained faithful to her husband and patiently bore her cross.

Nabal's servants respected Abigail and went to her with their troubles. They trusted her wisdom and ability to help them. Realizing that she must act quickly to avert the destruction of her husband's home, Abigail decided to meet David personally and try to pacify him. She knew that it would have been futile to lay her plans before Nabal. David was on his way to take revenge on Nabal. But

Abigail pleaded with him that he should refrain from doing anything sinful that would bring him into disfavor with God. She spoke as though she were to blame for Nabal's rude act (vv. 24, 28). With remarkable tact and skill, she reasoned with David and influenced him to take no action against Nabal. David was grateful for her good counsel.

5. Abigail had helped both Nabal and David. She had not deceived her husband but had acted for his best interests. She wisely waited until he was sober before she tried to explain her actions to him. Her report probably aroused his anger to such a pitch that he died from a stroke. Thus the Lord mercifully terminated Abigail's unhappy first marriage and cleared the way so that she could become David's wife. David was also unmarried at that time. Abigail can teach women who are unhappily married that the Lord is not ignorant of their plight.

Bathsheba

6. The story that tells us how Bathsheba became David's wife is one of the saddest chapters of the Bible. Participants may be familiar with the biblical account; if not, the group leader may want to read or have read the entire story. In this story, we see David's idleness, which enabled Satan to tempt him with lust, his sin of adultery with Bathsheba, his vain attempts to hide his crime, his murder of Uriah, his long impenitence, and his confession of sin after Nathan had preached the Law to him.

With David's marriage to Bathsheba, sorrow and trouble entered his home, never to leave it. The child begotten in adultery died soon after birth. As He does us, God chastised David, sometimes even severely, in order to keep him a humble believer to his end. "Besides this, we have had earthly fathers who disciplined us and we respected them. Shall we not much more be subject to the Father of spirits and live? For they disciplined us for a short time as it seemed best to them, but He disciplines us for our good, that we may share His holiness. For the moment all discipline seems painful rather than pleasant, but later it yields the peaceful fruit of righteousness to those who have been trained by it" (Hebrews 12:9–11).

7. Bathsheba's later life furnishes a brighter chapter. She seems to have been David's favorite wife and to have held the influential position of queen. She became the happy mother of Solomon, who in many, although not all, ways became a worthy successor to David. The Lord Himself designated that Solomon should be the next king (1 Chronicles 22:8–10). The honor greater than Solomon's respect for his mother is that God allowed her to become an ancestress of Christ (Matthew 1:6).

Other Women of That Period

8. In addition to Michal, Abigail, and Bathsheba, the Bible lists Ahinoam, Maacah, Haggith, Abital, and Eglah as David's wives. This list does not include David's concubines.

9. Solomon demonstrated God's wisdom in distinguishing between guilt-ridden jealousy and a truthful mother's self-sacrificial love.

10. Solomon undoubtedly married the Egyptian princess for political reasons; such a marriage would forge an alliance between Israel and Egypt. Solomon honored his Egyptian bride by building a beautiful cedar-lined palace, much like his throne hall and his own palace, for her to live in (1 Kings 7:8).

11. The famous Queen of Sheba's home was in southwestern Arabia, probably the modern Yemen. She was wise, rich, influential, and eager to grow in knowledge. Her long journey of hundreds of miles across the desert was a tremendous undertaking for a woman. Apparently she became a convert to the Hebrew religion. The queen wisely praised the Lord God of Israel for Solomon's great wisdom (1 Kings 10:9). In Matthew 12:42, Jesus indicates that the queen will stand in judgment against unbelievers on the Last Day.

12. Solomon's many wives brought along with them their many gods. With this false worship came immoral living. As Christians, we should be careful whose company we keep so that we do not become hardened in sin and make shipwreck of our faith (see 1 Timothy 1:18–19).

Jezebel

Not all the women described in the Bible were faithful, God-fearing servants of the Lord. Among the Bible "bad girls" are Jezebel in the Old Testament and Herodias in the New Testament. The two were so much alike that what may be said of the one applies equally to the other. In this session, we will look only at Jezebel, who besides Herodias is perhaps the most wicked woman in the Bible.

The Pagan Queen of Israel

13. As his name indicates, Jezebel's father, Ethbaal, was a worshiper of Baal, the god of the Phoenicians and Canaanites. The female counterpart of that male god was Asherah, or Astarte, who was worshiped with wild, sensual orgies in "groves."

Jezebel's marriage to Ahab is not surprising. She married him for political reasons. Ahab was dissolute, weak in character and morals, and an apostate from the religion of the Lord. Jezebel became his evil genius and led him from bad to worse. She won Ahab over to her gods, had him erect a large statue of Baal at Samaria, and fed 850 prophets of Baal and Astarte at their court. Jezebel induced Ahab to introduce Baal worship in the northern kingdom of Israel (1 Kings 16:31–32). For her part, she fostered the cult of Astarte (1 Kings 16:33; 18:19b). The worship of these two idols went hand in hand, and Jezebel's powerful religious influence in Israel was felt throughout the land.

14. Jezebel was determined to remove and destroy the old religion completely, and she showed no scruples in her choice of tactics. Her crimes included murdering Israelite prophets (1 Kings 18:13) and supporting 850 false prophets of Baal and Asherah (v. 19). The man whom Jezebel hated the most was Elijah, the great prophet of the Lord. Her inability to liquidate him enraged this bloodthirsty villain.

15. Jezebel remained unconvinced by the mighty display of Jehovah's power on Mount Carmel (1 Kings 18 and 19:1–2). Her

anger knew no bounds when Ahab told her about Elijah's slaughter of her pagan prophets. Defiantly, she showed her contempt for God's prophet, even attempting to slay Elijah. Since she completely dominated Ahab, Elijah refused to stay in the land in which God wanted him to labor.

Nevertheless, God promised that a remnant of true believers would remain (the "seven thousand" of 1 Kings 19:18). Jesus also imparts comfort to us today with His promise that the "gates of hell shall not prevail" against His Church (Matthew 16:18).

The Murderess of Naboth

16. According Mosaic Law, the Israelites were unable to sell their inherited property and had to keep it within their families (1 Kings 21:3; Numbers 36:7). Thus, Naboth could not legally sell his vineyard to Ahab. Note Ahab's reaction: "[he] went into his house vexed and sullen" (1 Kings 19:4).

17. Jezebel had no respect for the laws of God or of her country. In order to obtain Naboth's vineyard for her husband, Ahab, she misused a law that stipulated that a person should be executed for blasphemy (Leviticus 24:16). According to 2 Kings 9:26, she also had Naboth's sons killed, so that there would be no heirs. Then the ownerless property could be claimed by her husband, the king.

In this whole sordid ordeal, Jezebel broke the first commandment by placing herself above God, the second by misusing the Lord's name, the fourth by undermining God-given authority, the fifth by committing murder, the seventh by stealing, and the eighth by bearing false witness against her neighbor. We can only surmise that Ahab, being weak and self-absorbed, capitulated to her plans out of self-interest. After Naboth's death, Ahab meekly obeyed his cruel wife's commands and secured Naboth's vineyard for himself.

Impenitent to Her End

18. Read 2 Kings 9:30–37. Jezebel had been punished through the death of her husband (1 Kings 22:34–38) and the loss of her children (2 Kings 9:24–26). But she did not repent of her sins. Even when the destroyer of her family, Jehu, God's avenger, had caught up with her, she thought that with her charms and defiance she

could gain a reprieve for herself. But her hour had struck. She could not have died a more horrible and shameful death.

God, however, did not desire that even Jezebel die apart from His saving grace; He wanted her also to seek Him in repentant faith (2 Peter 3:9). Her sinful refusal of His love and forgiveness, proclaimed through His prophets, is the cause of her eternity now spent in hell. As Christians, having been baptized and knowing God's Word of Law and Gospel, we should make the most of the Lord's grace by hearing and reading His Word and frequently receiving the Lord's Supper. Through these means, God applies to us the forgiveness of sins won for us by Christ and enables us to live lives pleasing to Him.

19. Jezebel promoted the false religions of Baal and Asherah. Like all false religions, these could not coexist with the religion of the one true God. As Professor Brighton seems to suggest, already in our day we see a religion of syncretism, which would make all religions equal—except that of orthodox Christianity.

Allow participants to answer how we can today guard against this modern Jezebel. One way is to commit ourselves to Bible study and Bible memorization. Another is to carry out an active program of sharing our faith and evangelization, so that more people of our world come to know the saving truth of our Redeemer, Jesus Christ.

Other Women of That Period

20. Here we have another case, like that of David and Bathsheba's first child, of temporal punishment for sins that have been forgiven. We cannot help but feel sorry for Jeroboam's wife. The words of 1 Kings 14:13 seem to indicate that she was a pious woman and had exerted a good influence on her sick child.

Allow participants to discuss what comfort believing parents have at the death of a child, especially the many rich and comforting passages of Scripture relating to Holy Baptism. Encourage reflection on how they individually and as a congregation can work together to provide help to parents and children who lose loved ones, especially small children.

21. The beautiful story of the faithful widow of Zarephath (1 Kings 17:8–24) serves to counterbalance the sad and sordid story

of Jezebel. The pagan widow came to have a strong faith in God, which was reflected in how she treated the Lord's servant and obeyed the Word of the Lord. She was hospitable, unselfish, and willing to share her last food with a stranger. From Elijah she learned to rely on the Lord for every need.

The two miracles the Lord worked through Elijah for the widow were the abundant provision of flour and oil (1 Kings 17:14–16) and the raising from the dead of the widow's son (vv. 22–23). Note how highly Jesus honored the widow's memory (Luke 4:25–26). In Luke's Gospel, the widow's faith and that of Naaman the Syrian (v. 27) emphasize God's grace and favor being extended even to the Gentiles.

The Shunammite Woman

The story of the Shunammite woman is a wonderful portrayal of good works enabled by faith in our gracious God. The Shunammite displays Hebrew hospitality, faithfulness, and concern for strangers. The study of her life recorded in the Bible offers an opportunity to discuss the need and importance of showing hospitality, which is also a Christian virtue. The Shunammite's care and concern for God's prophet also allows us to see how we should care for our pastors, who likewise speak God's Word to us today.

A Woman of Hospitality

22. Shunem was southeast of Nazareth, near Mount Tabor. Here, in the home of a pious couple, the prophet Elisha could rest and enjoy their unselfish hospitality. The Shunammite woman proved her faith by her deeds, exhibited contentment in her circumstances, appreciated God's blessings, and showed that she relied upon God to help her out of her troubles. Verse 9 shows she recognized that Elisha was "a holy man of God." This is the only place in Scripture where a prophet is called "holy." Undoubtedly, she was able to recognize this about Elisha because he spoke God's Word.

23. The Shunammite did all she could to make Elisha's hard life as pleasant as possible. She offered him all the comforts her home could give. She conceived a plan, which she discussed with her husband. Jointly they agreed to add a little room to their house, which she furnished comfortably so that Elisha could relax there whenever he passed through Shunem.

Allow participants to discuss how we, like the Shunammite, are given the task and enabled by God to provide for the needs of pastors, teachers, and other church workers. Go further by discussing concrete ways in which this is being done or should be done.

24. Elisha was grateful for this lady's thoughtfulness and hospitality, and he tried his best to reward her. He knew that God would, in answer to his prayer, give the woman whatever she

needed. But this woman was not selfish and greedy. With her answer (v. 13), she meant to say that she was content with what she had. (See 1 Timothy 6:6.)

Through Gehazi, his servant, Elisha discovered that a great sorrow was gnawing at her heart. She had no child, her husband was old (v. 14), and she had given up all hopes of becoming a mother. Elisha told her she would have a son. This news seemed to be too good to be true, but it wasn't. God gave her a son in answer to Elisha's promise and prayer (vv. 15–17).

As time permits, allow participants to read what the Bible teaches about hospitality and its reward: Job 31:32; Matthew 10:41; Romans 12:13; and Hebrews 13:2.

A Woman Who Believed in God's Promise

25. God sent this woman a severe trial to test her faith. The child she loved so dearly suddenly became ill, perhaps from sunstroke, and died. Nothing is said about the grief of this mother. She seems to have kept that deep in her heart. She did not complain or permit her sorrow to stun her senses. She had a strong faith and believed that God would help her through His prophet. Therefore, she hurried to Mount Carmel (about 16 miles away, a four-hour journey) to find Elisha.

Elisha wondered why the Shunammite woman had come to see him. Her heart was too heavy to tell him her sorrow, and God gave him no direct revelation. The woman's words reveal the strength of her faith. She did not lie to him when she told him that everything was well (v. 26). She believed that what God had done was for her good (Romans 8:28).

Allow participants to discuss to whom we should turn when we are faced with sadness, illness, or grief. Among those who can help us during these times are Christian family members, friends, and members of our congregation, as well as our pastor and other church workers.

26. Through Elisha, God performed one of the most remarkable miracles recorded in the Bible. Elisha laid himself upon the boy, and God restored the boy to life. With admirable calmness and humility, the Shunammite thanked Elisha by bowing to the ground.

Then she took her son into her arms and withdrew to her own room, there to thank God with all her heart.

Allow participants to discuss how we can show thankfulness to our Christian brothers and sisters when they have helped us during our times of need. Solicit practical examples, such as a thank-you note, telephone call, returned favor, and so on.

A Woman Who Experienced God's Help

27. Sometime later, God again tested this woman's faith. Elisha told her to go to another country while a famine was raging in Israel. The famine would last seven years. Elisha did not want her to suffer while God was punishing the wicked Israelites. In obedience to God's Word, she went to the country of the Philistines. It seems that her husband was dead at that time.

Allow participants to discus how their congregation currently provides for or could be of temporal assistance to congregational and community members during times of need. Examples include a food or clothing bank, financial assistance during peak utility bill seasons, assistance with parochial school tuition, or volunteering at a homeless shelter.

28. After seven years, the woman returned with her son to her old home in accordance with the prophet's instructions. But now new troubles awaited her. During her absence, her property had been confiscated by the government. She was now without a home and income. But she did not lose the courage of faith. In His gracious providence, God so arranged matters that Gehazi was at the king's court at the very time she arrived to make her plea. Gehazi had just finished telling the king what Elisha had done for this woman. This so impressed the king that he immediately gave orders to have all her property restored to her. That is the last we hear of this God-fearing, kindhearted woman, who served God by honoring, helping, and obeying the Lord's prophet.

Allow participants to suggest ways that they could advocate for the poor, the homeless, or those who otherwise might not receive fair treatment under the law. Opportunities for assistance might include public housing education, free classes on budgeting and credit, or pro bono work on behalf of the poor by Christian attorneys.

Other Women of That Period

29. The story of the widow in 2 Kings 4:1–7 also shows how wonderfully God provides for our temporal needs through the resources that we already have. He can make a little go far.

Allow participants to suggest resources that they or their congregation already have that could be put to good use in service to the community.

30. This story of a little Israelite girl is a good example of testifying about one's faith and doing personal mission work even under the most adverse conditions.

Our God-given faith enables us to share our testimony about God's grace in Jesus Christ with others. Allow participants to list the people they will pray to have the opportunity to share their faith with, such as family members, friends, co-workers, and so on.

31. As is sometimes the case: like mother, like daughter. It may be sufficient to show how much Athaliah was like her mother, Jezebel. Such examples in the Bible should serve to warn Christian parents against modeling improper behavior and language at home and to encourage them to set an example for their children to follow. "Train up a child in the way he should go; even when he is old he will not depart from it" (Proverbs 22:6).

32. Apparently, Hezekiah's wife made no good impression upon their son, Manasseh. Care should be taken here not to give the impression that parents are totally responsible for the outward behavior of their adult children. However, parental influence does play a strong role.

33. The case of Huldah is similar to that of Deborah (Judges 4) in that she was called a prophetess. Scripture does not record the responsibilities of these special women. On occasion, they appear to speak the Word of God to individuals or groups; perhaps they were also considered leaders of women. In any case, prophetesses were rare and seem to be the exception rather than the rule. No Bible passage establishes an office of prophetess.

Esther

The Book of Esther, the last of the historical books of the Old Testament, portrays the remarkable story of Esther. The book is too long to be studied in detail, but participants should be encouraged to read it at home in its entirety. The chief purpose of this session is to study the life and character of Esther and note how she played her role as queen of Persia to the benefit of God's people.

Esther Becomes Queen

34. The first chapter explains how the way was prepared for Esther to become queen of the Persian Empire. We are not interested in Vashti at this time; her story should be treated separately (see Other Women of That Period below).

Ahasuerus has been identified with King Xerxes, the powerful Persian ruler (480–465 BC), whose attempted invasion of Greece ended in disaster for the Persians (at Thermopylae). This probably happened during the four years that elapsed between the demotion of Vashti and the coronation of Esther (see Esther 1:3; 2:16). Shushan, also called Susa, was the capital of the Persian Empire. It lay about 200 miles north of the Persian Gulf.

The Bible does not say how Mordecai felt about Esther being taken to Ahasuerus; she certainly would have become merely one woman in his vast harem. Though it's unlikely Esther or Mordecai had a choice in the matter, perhaps Mordecai could already see God's hand providing for Esther and putting her in a position of potential influence. While Esther's Persian name means "star," her given Hebrew name was *Hadassah*, which means "myrtle."

35. Esther did not reveal that she was Jewish because Mordecai had forbidden her to do so (2:20). He evidently feared that this knowledge might prejudice the king against her. He kept as close to the palace as possible so that he could learn how Esther fared at court.

Esther's People Threatened with Destruction

36. Haman was an Amalekite, a member of a tribe that was an ancient foe of the Israelites (1 Samuel 15:8). Haman was promoted by the king to a position of highest honor and power. He hated the Jews, and particularly Mordecai, because they refused to do reverence and submit to this enemy of their race (Esther 3:5–6). Craving revenge, he persuaded the king to sign a decree that all the Jews should be destroyed (vv. 7–11). In giving his consent to this evil plan, Ahasuerus did not know that he had decreed the death of Esther. Judas, of course, also betrayed a Jew, our Savior, Jesus Christ, by accepting a bribe of 30 pieces of silver (see Matthew 26:14–16).

37. Mordecai, horror-stricken when he read the decree, urged Esther to go to the king and plead for the lives of her people. Esther was afraid to do this because she had not been called by the king for a long time. To go to him unbidden might arouse his anger and cost her life (Esther 4:11). Mordecai warned her that if she would not take the risk, she would perish, and God would find other means for saving the Jews (v. 14). Esther was now willing to risk her life by making the attempt (v. 16).

Esther Saves Her People from Destruction

38. God gave success to Esther's plan so that the king received her kindly (5:2). She knew that she had to proceed with caution and tact. First, she had to win the king completely to her side before she could accuse his favorite of a crime. She invited the king and Haman to a feast that she planned to give (5:4). On this occasion, she did not consider it wise to present her petition. Therefore, she invited the king and Haman to a second banquet the next day (5:8). Clearly, Esther was waiting for the right time and circumstances to make her accusation.

39. Esther patiently waited until the second feast—by which time Ahasuerus was eager to grant her request—to expose Haman's plot. Esther presented him to the king as the destroyer of her people (7:1–6). The king now was angry with Haman and in his rage, which was always uncontrollable, had him hanged on the gallows that Haman had prepared for Mordecai (vv. 7–10).

But the decree of death that hung over the Jews was still in force. The law could not be annulled (8:8; see also Daniel 6:8). Something had to be done to prevent the enemies of the Jews from carrying out the provisions of the law. Esther induced the king to publish another decree that would give the Jews the right to defend themselves and fight for their lives (8:7–11). This decree frightened their enemies and held them in check (v. 17).

Esther Is Honored

40. Everywhere there was feasting and rejoicing over the victory of Esther and Mordecai (8:16–17). Because the king's edict now gave the Jews the ability to defend themselves, they did so with great boldness, which incited fear among their enemies (9:2–16).

41. The Jews celebrated their victory with a two-day festival known since that time as Purim (9:18–22). The name *pur* in Hebrew means "lot" (v. 24; *purim* is the Hebrew plural). Esther 9:21–28 shows how the festival was celebrated in Esther's day.

To this day, Jewish people annually observe the anniversary of the deliverance of their ancestors in Persia with joyous festivities. While the household is seated at the table for the festival meal, the father reads portions of the story of Esther, and the members of the family hiss whenever Haman's name is mentioned. The day (in February) is celebrated with joy and an exchange of gifts.

42. Encourage participants to list the faith-filled deeds of Mordecai and Esther found in the Book of Esther. Among the many examples are Mordecai's refusal to bow down to Haman and Esther's risking of her own life to save the lives of her people. Although the Book of Esther does not mention God's name, throughout its pages we see His hand of providence protecting and providing for His covenant people.

Other Women in the Book of Esther

43. We meet Queen Vashti in Esther 1. She may have been in the right by refusing to gratify the wishes of a drunken king and his court. But such a usurpation of authority could not be tolerated. Although the Scripture does not indicate this, we can assume that

Vashti may have been killed or banished for what would have amounted to a great embarrassment to Ahasuerus.

44. Zeresh originally supported her husband's opposition to Mordecai and with his friends even suggested building a gallows for him (Esther 5:14). However, when it became apparent that her husband was about to lose favor with the king, she became scornful and a doomsayer (6:13).

Allow participants to discuss the importance of consistency in dealing with loved ones, particularly when it comes to values and advice.